DEMOCRACY

DEMOCRACY

ODYSSEYS

ANNE FITZPATRICK

CREATIVE EDUCATION · CREATIVE PAPERBACKS

Published by Creative Education and Creative Paperbacks
P.O. Box 227, Mankato, Minnesota 56002
Creative Education and Creative Paperbacks are imprints of
The Creative Company
www.thecreativecompany.us

Book design by Blue Design (www.bluedes.com)
Art direction by Rita Marshall
Printed in China

Photographs by Alamy (ALIKI SAPOUNTZI/aliki image library, Michael Dwyer, Bill Howe, Lebrecht Music and Arts Photo Library, North Wind Picture Archives, Pictorial Press, Christopher Pillitz, Popperfoto, Stock Connection/Rob Crandall), Corbis (Archivo Iconografico, Armin Weigel/epa, Bettmann, Burstein Collection, Flip Schulke), Getty Images (ADRIAN DENNIS, AFP, ROBYN BECK, Blue Line Pictures, The Image Bank, HECTOR MATA, Mario Tama, Stringer, FARZANA WAHIDY/Stringer)

Library of Congress Cataloging-in-Publication Data
Fitzpatrick, Anne.
Democracy / Anne Fitzpatrick.
p. cm. — (Odysseys in government)
Includes bibliographical references and index.
Summary: An examination of the democratic form of government, including its basic ideologies and structure, its best-known leaders throughout history, and countries affected by its system of rule.

ISBN 978-1-60818-724-9 (hardcover)
ISBN 978-1-62832-320-7 (pbk)
ISBN 978-1-56660-759-9 (eBook)
1. Democracy. 2. Representative government and representation.

JC423.F636 2016
321.8—dc23 2015048534

CCSS: RI.8.1, 2, 3, 4; RI.9-10.1, 2, 3, 4; RI.11-12.1, 2, 3, 4; RH.6-8.1, 4, 5, 7; RH.9-10.1, 3, 4

First Edition HC 9 8 7 6 5 4 3 2 1
First Edition PBK 9 8 7 6 5 4 3 2 1

CONTENTS

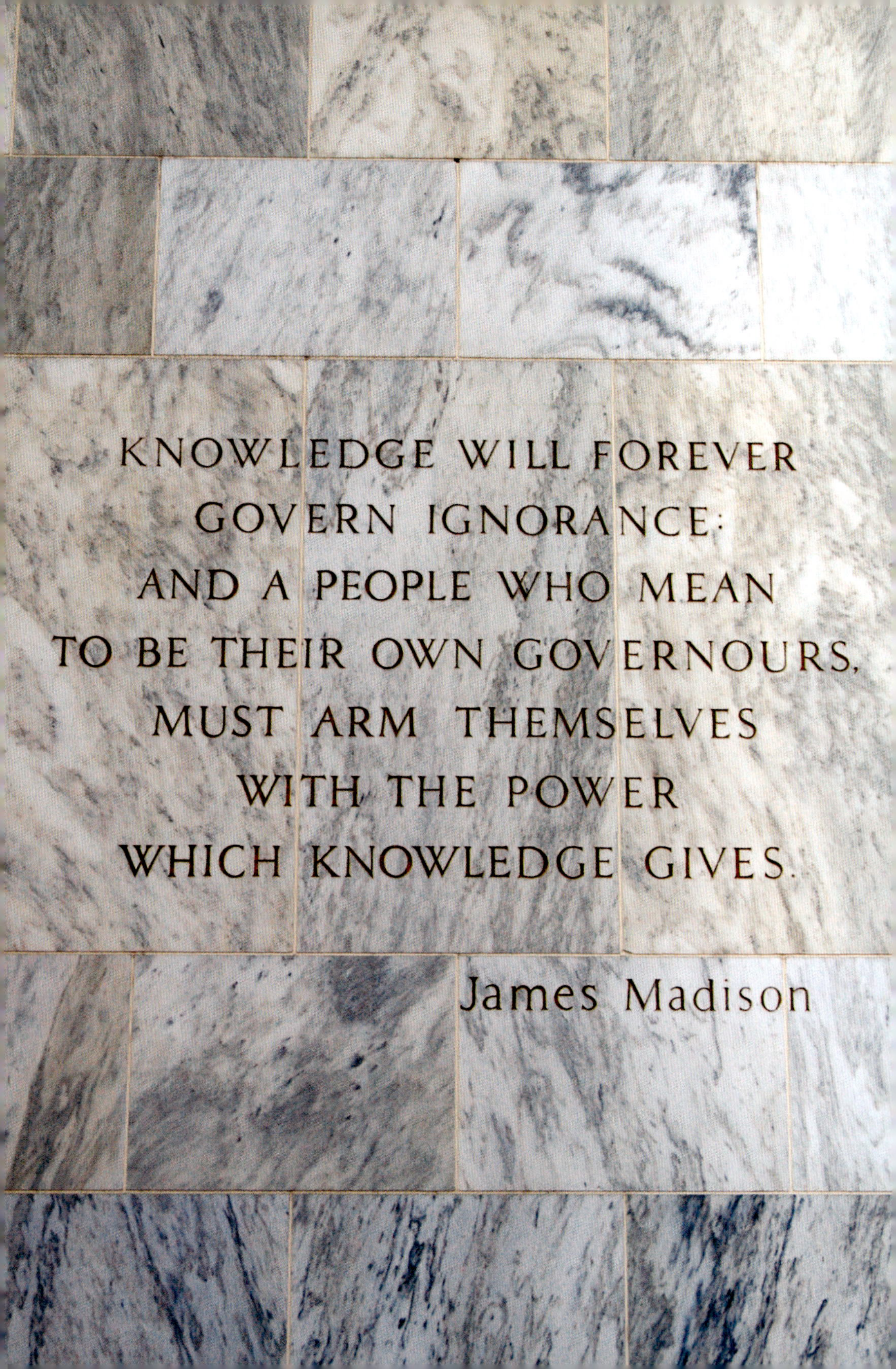
KNOWLEDGE WILL FOREVER
GOVERN IGNORANCE:
AND A PEOPLE WHO MEAN
TO BE THEIR OWN GOVERNOURS,
MUST ARM THEMSELVES
WITH THE POWER
WHICH KNOWLEDGE GIVES.
James Madison

Power to the People

A government is like the tiller on a ship. It is the system by which the life of a community is steered. A ship without a tiller might get pulled out to sea, or it might never get out of the harbor. Likewise, a community without a government will be at the mercy of its most powerful members or will be too disorganized to get things done, such as building roads and paying police officers.

OPPOSITE: A quotation on the exterior of the James Madison Memorial Building in Washington, D.C.

Who gets to hold the tiller and how they use it to steer the ship depends on the form of government. In a democracy, everyone gets to steer. The term *democracy* comes from a Greek word that means "rule by the people." In a true direct democracy, all of the citizens participate in making the laws. For example, the citizens of Switzerland often vote on whether to accept or reject new laws. But most democracies are too large and complicated for everyone to get together to make all the decisions. So the people elect representatives to make the decisions for them. This is called a representative democracy, or democratic **republic**. The United States and Canada are representative democracies. Representatives serve for only short terms before they have to be reelected. Their decisions must make a majority of the people happy, or the people will elect someone else. In this way, the power stays in the hands of the people.

Keeping power in the hands of the people is the goal of a democratic form of government. Regular elections are one way to give power to the people. Another way is to spread power among many different government officials, so that they have to work together to get things done. For example, laws that affect the entire U.S. must be agreed upon by a majority of the representatives of every state. That way, the people of one state cannot always get their way at the expense of the others. In the Netherlands and Sweden, several political parties with different views often have to cooperate in order to pass laws.

Letting one person or group of people have too much power is a concern in a democracy, because people with too much power tend to use it to get more power, and then the government is not in the hands of the people anymore. Democracies often address this by separating the different functions of government into independent branches of government. Each branch then has a limited amount of power. Moreover, each branch can keep an eye on the other branches to make sure they are all acting in the best interest of the people.

Democracies often separate the legislative and executive functions of government into different branches. The legislative branch, or legislature, is responsible for making the laws, and the executive branch, which usually consists of a president or prime minister and the people who work for him or her, is responsible for carrying those laws out. For example, the legislature might pass a law that all citizens should get free education. The executive branch would then hire teachers, rent space for classes, and make all of the little decisions that the legislature did not put in the law, such as what subjects to teach and how long the school day should last.

In a democracy, the legislative branch usually is an assembly of representatives, each of whom is elected by people in a different part of the country. The head of the executive branch is either elected by the whole country, as in the U.S. and South Korea, or is chosen by the legislature, as in Canada and India. The things the executive can do are limited by the rules set for it by the legislature. On the other hand, if the legislature passes unjust laws, the executive can refuse to carry them out. For example, U.S. president James Madison (1751–1836) prevented Congress from giving special privileges to certain churches in 1811, arguing that this endangered religious freedom. In this way, the two branches limit each other's power.

Another important function of democratic government is the judicial function. This includes deciding disagreements among citizens, hearing **petitions**, and **trying** and punishing people accused of violating the law. These things are essential to a democracy

James Madison, fourth U.S. president

Is Democracy Enough?

One of the first people to use the word "democracy" was the Greek philosopher Aristotle (384–322 B.C.). He studied in Athens at the academy founded by Plato (c. 428–347 B.C.), another philosopher. After Plato's death, Aristotle opened his own school. Because he liked to walk while he taught, Aristotle's school became known as the peripatetic, or walking, school.

Aristotle believed that democracy was the best form of government, but he did not think that democracy alone was enough to ensure good government. Those who govern must have skill, wisdom, knowledge, and experience; just because men are all equal in the eyes of the law does not mean they are all equally able to rule. For Aristotle, a democracy could be ruled by a few people, as long as everyone agreed to be ruled by them, and as long as the people who ruled did not stay in power forever. He also worried that if government officers were chosen by election, people would vote for the richest or most powerful candidate, rather than the wisest. He thought it would be better to choose among qualified candidates by lottery!

because they give everyone a chance to be heard by the government.

Democracies usually carry out these functions through courts presided over by judges. A judicial branch that is independent of the other branches of government can ensure that the rights of the people under the laws are protected, even if it is the government from whom they need protection. When the legislature passes an unfair law or the executive enforces a law in an unfair way, the people can turn to the courts for help. In Germany, for example, the highest court can review any law passed by the legislature or any act carried out by a member of the government to make sure that it does not violate the German constitution. In 1987, the court found that the government acted unconstitutionally when it took land away from a farmer and gave it to an automobile manufacturer.

In order for the separation of legislative, executive, and judicial functions to work, government must be carried out by the rule of law. This means that the government exercises its power according to written laws that were adopted through proper procedures, such as a vote by the legislature. The executive cannot throw someone in jail unless the law says he or she can. The legislature must have written and voted for a law that says if anyone robs a bank, for example, he or she can be put in jail. Then the judicial branch makes sure that the executive was following the law when it decided to put the person in jail.

Written laws adopted through established procedures increase the **transparency** of government. It is important that people have accurate, **unbiased**, and **uncensored** information about how the government works and what it is doing so that they can participate in government in an informed way. For example, if citizens who care about clean water do not know that the government gave a factory permission to pollute a river, they will not be able to

U.S. president Richard Nixon's resignation, 1974

try to change the law by talking to their representatives or petitioning a court.

Transparency also makes government officials accountable for their actions, which limits their power and ensures that they will try to act in the best interest of the people they govern. If government officials know that people will find out and get upset when they allow a factory to pollute a river, they may not do it. Or they may think they are actually acting in the best interest of the people when they give the factory permission to pollute, and it is only when the citizens find out and complain that they realize this is not what people want. A lack of transparency can bring democratic leaders down; U.S. president Richard Nixon (1913–94), for example, fell from power because of secretive (and illegal) political actions in the early 1970s.

Some of the laws in a democracy may form a constitution. A constitution is a set of laws or ideas, such as equal rights, that are considered more important than regular laws. Extraordinary measures are required to change them, such as **unanimous** or near-unanimous consent of the people or their representatives. Because not everyone always agrees on how things should be done, democracies are usually ruled by the majority—the person with the most votes gets elected, or a law is passed if more than 50 percent of the legislature votes for it. There is therefore a danger that the majority might abuse its power over the minority. Thomas Jefferson (1743–1826), one of the founders of democracy in the U.S., once said, "A democracy is nothing more than mob rule, where 51 percent of the people may take away the rights of the other 49."

A constitution protects the minority by setting aside the things that are so important that even if most people want to change them, they cannot. It creates an important limitation on the power of the government. A constitution usually includes the basic organizational laws of the government, such as which governmental powers are exercised by which parts of government, and a list of important rights, such as the right to equality and the right to free expression.

Protecting Rights and Righting Wrongs

In a democracy, the people are **sovereign**. This means that, in general, the government cannot interfere with their freedom to live and work where and how they choose. There is an assumption, however, that everyone who lives in a democracy has agreed to live by its laws. That is why the government can require people to pay taxes and put people who commit

OPPOSITE: An eagle, the U.S. symbol for freedom, and the national flag atop the Eisenhower Executive Office Building in Washington, D.C.

crimes in jail. But the assumption goes both ways: in return for citizens' agreement to obey the laws, the government agrees to protect their rights.

For example, democracies often guarantee the right to freely practice one's religion. This is true even in countries that have an official state church, such as the Church of England, or an official religion, such as Catholicism in Costa Rica. British and Costa Rican citizens are not required to be members of the Church of England or of the Catholic Church, and they do not have to obey the rules of those religions. Other countries, such as Australia and Turkey, have not established an official religion and try to treat all religions equally.

Making sure that people's rights will be protected is very important because governments, even democratic governments, usually are much more powerful than in-

Who Are "the People"?

Early democracies differed from modern ones with regard to who was allowed to participate in government. Prior to the 19th century, only 5 percent of the British population over the age of 20 could vote; voting was limited to free men who owned property. In the U.S., nonwhite men were not given the right to vote until 1870, and women could not vote until 1920.

Despite democracy's emphasis on freedom and individual rights, the citizens of many democracies once owned slaves. Although the Athenian practice of enslaving people who could not pay their debts was abolished in the sixth century B.C., people who were captured in wars and children born into slavery were still enslaved. Beginning in the 15th century, African people were captured and taken to Europe and the Americas, where they were sold to landowners and forced to work. The practice was not abolished until the 19th century.

Even after slavery was abolished and equality was made universal, it was often difficult for women and nonwhites to get elected. Creating truly representative governments has been a slow process. Even today, many democratic governments do not accurately reflect the diversity of the population.

Suffragists protesting president Woodrow Wilson's views in 1916

dividuals. If the government decides to put someone in prison or take his or her property, there is little anyone can do to stop it. There is a danger that the government will abuse that power and act unfairly, such as by imprisoning people without proving that they actually committed the crime for which they were arrested. Democracies protect people from such abuses by requiring that the government follow certain procedures whenever it takes freedom or property away from a citizen. These requirements are collectively known as the right to due process.

What constitutes due process may be different in different democracies. For example, in the U.S., due process requires the police to tell a suspect they are arresting that he or she has the right to remain silent. But in Japan, suspects are told that they have a right to tell their story. Although the law protects their right to remain silent as well, the emphasis is on giving the accused the opportunity to talk. Despite these differences, all democracies require some kind of trial that meets certain standards of fairness whenever someone is accused of a crime.

Democracies protect rights such as freedom of religion and the right to due process because they are seen as basic and natural rights with which everyone is born. But some rights are also important to protect because democracy cannot function properly without them. The freedom to think, speak, write, and otherwise express oneself—in private, on a street corner, or through the press or other media—is one such right. People must be able to freely discuss political issues in order to participate in democratic government. Thus, in a democracy, the government does not censor news articles before they can be published or decide which movies can be released in theaters, even when the articles or movies are critical of the government.

Freedom of assembly is also essential to democracy. It means that people have a right to get together and organize in any way they choose. In many undemocratic countries, the government bans certain organizations, such as rival political parties, because they may be a threat to the government's control. There is power in numbers, and that makes organized groups of people dangerous to a government that is trying to keep all of the power for itself.

But in a democracy, the people are supposed to have the power. If they want to organize a new political party in order to get different government officials elected, that is their right. They are doing exactly what people in a democracy are supposed to be doing. The formation of political parties and other organizations may even be encouraged. For example, when Great Britain's Labour Party formed in 1900, the party in power, the Liberals, not only did not try to prevent it but cooperated with members of the new party to pass laws.

One of the most important rights that democracies protect for their citizens is the right to equality. Equality is protected in many ways. In elections, each citizen has one vote; even if one person is smarter or wealthier than another, their votes count equally. Equal protection also

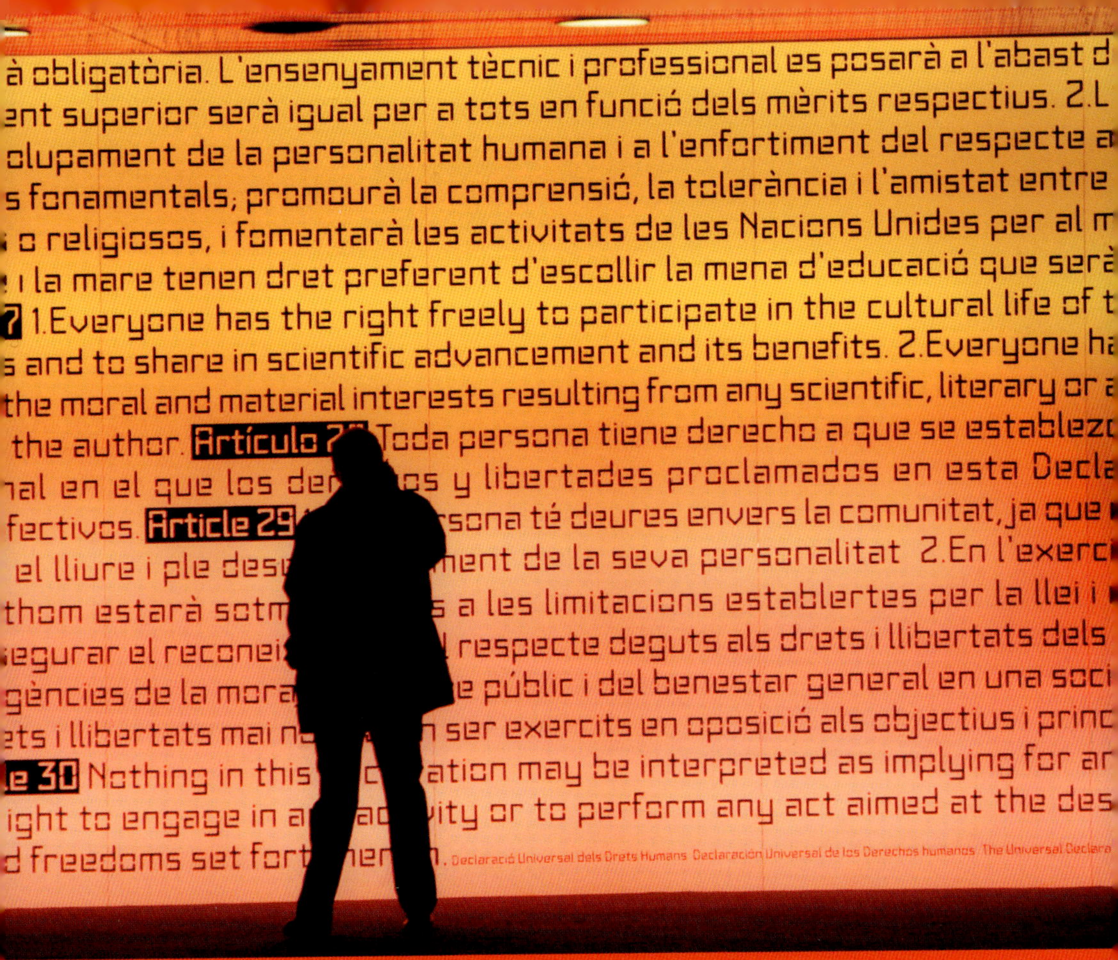

International Human Rights

In 1948, in the shadow of World War II and its atrocities, the United Nations unanimously adopted the Universal Declaration of **Human Rights**. There are no legal consequences for countries that violate its principles, so many countries ignore it. Nonetheless, it announces ideals toward which all nations should strive.

The declaration states that "all human beings are born free and equal in dignity and rights," and "everyone is entitled to all the rights and freedoms … without distinction of any kind, such as race, color, sex, language, religion, political or other opinion, national or social origin, property, birth, or other status."

The rights and freedoms established by the declaration include important principles of democracy, such as the right to life, liberty, and security; freedom of religion; freedom of opinion and expression, including the right to seek and receive information and ideas; the right to peaceful assembly; the right to a fair, impartial, and public trial in criminal cases; the freedom to own property; and the freedom to participate in government.

means that the government enforces laws equally upon everyone. Even government officials are not above the law; if they commit a crime, they must be punished. Democratic governments may also protect the right to equality by passing laws that forbid discrimination. For example, they may make it illegal for a company to refuse to hire women, or for a landlord to refuse to rent an apartment to people of a different race.

Equality is particularly important to the proper functioning of a democracy because democracies are based on the idea that the government belongs to everyone. When people are not equal, they cannot participate equally in government. But in most democracies, there is no right to an equal amount of wealth. Sometimes this can get in the way of true political equality. When a few people are much wealthier than everyone else, they have a lot more power. For example, running for election usually requires a lot of money—people will not vote for you if they do not know who you are, and advertising is expensive. As a result, it is easier for a very wealthy person to get elected or to influence the outcome of an election.

At the other extreme, poverty can make it difficult for people to participate in government. When you are too busy worrying about how you are going to eat, you cannot pay much attention to what the government is doing and how you would like it to change.

Someone without much money is unlikely to run for office or to petition the courts because those things are often expensive and time-consuming. Thus, the voices of the poor may rarely be heard by the government, although they technically have as much of a right to speak as anyone else.

There will always be economic inequalities in a democracy, because one of the rights that democracies protect is the right to property. In some forms of government, such as communism, no one can own property because everything is shared by everyone. But in a democracy, citizens have the right to own things. The government will help them protect that right; for example, the government will arrest a person who steals other people's property. Even the government cannot take people's property away unless it has a very good reason to do so and pays the property owner for the loss.

There are some ways that democracies can try to even the playing field for rich and poor people who want to participate in government. For example, New Zealand and Israel have laws in place that give people who are running for office a certain amount of free advertising. They also distribute money to political parties to use in their campaigns. Many countries, including Argentina and Japan, restrict how much money any one person or group can give to a candidate.

Giving poor people access to courts is a major concern in many democracies. Although a lawyer usually is not required in order to petition a court, not having a lawyer can be a major disadvantage. In the Netherlands, government-sponsored "legal aid" centers provide lawyers who charge different fees based on what each person can afford to pay. In the U.S., many lawyers volunteer their services for free to people in need, and there are legal aid centers run by private charities.

There are other ways that people participate in government for which unequal wealth does not matter. In some democracies, people can participate in government by serving on a **jury**. Being on a jury does not cost any money—in fact, people usually get paid for it. In modern democracies, voting does not require money, although this was not always the case. Prior to the 19th century, voting was usually limited to people who owned a certain amount of property. In the U.S. in the 19th and 20th centuries, some southern states passed laws requiring payment of a "poll tax" before one could vote in order to prevent black people—who were mostly poor at the time—from voting. Such laws were banned in 1964.

The Choice of Democracy

It is clear why a citizen would prefer democracy over other forms of government. The average person has more power and more freedom in a democracy than in any other type of government in history. Democracy also prevents the oppression and cruelty that are possible in governments in which one person or group has absolute power. But in many cases in history, people who were already in

OPPOSITE: Representatives in newly democratic Iraq, 2006

power or who had the opportunity to take all of the power for themselves, such as the wealthy **nobles** who founded democracy in ancient Greece or the revolutionaries who wrote the U.S. Constitution, decided to create democratic governments—by choice, and not because the people rose up and demanded it. Why would they do that?

One reason is that people who trust the government and are loyal to it are more motivated to defend it and have no reason to revolt against it. Thus, a democratic nation is a stronger nation. On the other hand, a nation that gives its people so much power is dependent upon people's satisfaction with their government. In difficult times, when people are deeply divided and mistrustful, the government may be unstable. For example, passionate disagreements over slavery in the U.S. caused a civil war that nearly split the nation apart in the 1860s. In the democratic republic that was set up in Germany after World War I, dissatisfaction with the terms of the treaty that ended the war and frustration after the country's economic collapse enabled Adolf Hitler (1889–1945) to establish a **dictatorship** in 1933.

Ideally, however, a healthy democratic government should be flexible enough that dissatisfaction and distrust can be expressed and addressed through the normal operation of democracy. A leader who is

German dictator Adolf Hitler

abusing his or her power can be voted out of office, with no need for revolution. Disagreements can be settled through the political and legislative process with no need for civil war.

Not only are wars less likely within a democracy, but they are also less likely between democracies. Some people believe that there has never been a war between two democracies. Others disagree; it depends on how one defines a democracy and how one defines a war. Nonetheless, it is certainly true that democracies are less likely to go to war with each other. Immanuel Kant (1724–1804), a German philosopher, wrote in his 1795 essay *Perpetual Peace: A Philosophical Sketch* that the culture of a democracy, in which people are accustomed to negotiating and compromising, makes democracies less likely to take military action. He notes two other reasons

OPPOSITE Philosopher Immanuel Kant

democracies are less likely to go to war: Democracies take longer to make decisions, making it difficult to act quickly, as is required in wartime. Secondly, it is the people who bear the economic and human costs of war; because leaders in a democracy are subject to political pressure from the people, they are less likely to start a war that will result in these costs.

Kant's arguments also highlight two of the drawbacks of democracy: **bureaucracy** and short-term thinking. Because they require input from a lot of different people, democracies use up a lot of time and resources to reach a decision that a king or dictator could make almost instantly. For example, in Switzerland, the process of enacting a new law takes at least a year—in some cases, it has taken as long as 12 years. But bureaucracy seems to be a necessary evil; it is better to decide things slowly if that

J. KANT.

Plato in Raphael's fresco *The School of Athens*

is what is required to have everyone agree on what to do.

In addition, because the leaders of a democracy serve limited terms in office before they must be reelected or replaced by someone else, democracies may become focused on short-term costs and benefits. A king, who leads for a lifetime, may be better able to plan ahead. Bureaucracy is one answer to the problem of short-term thinking; a government that acts slowly is more likely to plan ahead.

Plato, an ancient Greek philosopher, argued that democracy could not work because people were mostly ignorant, short-sighted, and selfish; democracy would be the "rule of opinion over knowledge." He thought that people should have some choice as to who their leaders were, but that the leaders should be chosen from a special class of wise "philosopher-kings." Some of the founders of democracy in the U.S. made similar arguments; they worried that most people were uneducated and would be easily misled by wily politicians. They considered having Congress elect the president instead of holding a general election by the people.

Swiss-French philosopher Jean-Jacques Rousseau (1712–78) had more faith in the average person. He thought that a democracy created the perfect balance of freedom and restraint that would enable each person to think for him- or herself. Rousseau believed that if people are given this freedom to think for themselves, they will want to do what is best for the whole community. Thus, people become less selfish when they are part of a democratic community. Others have argued that even when people in a democracy act selfishly, they balance each other out so that the best outcome for everyone results. Moreover, because it puts power in the hands of more people, democracy harnesses a broader range of knowledge and experience, which may result in wiser government.

In fact, people who live in democracies tend to be more educated than people in nondemocratic countries. It may be that people reach their greatest potential when they are given equality of opportunity, the freedom to choose their occupations, and the right to enjoy the fruits of their labors. It also has been shown that democratically governed countries are more prosperous than countries with nondemocratic governments. Health, education, average individual income, and other measures of personal development and well-being are better in democracies.

Although people as a whole tend to be better off in a democracy, there are often large differences in wealth among different groups of people within a democracy. Some argue that focusing on the ideals of equality and equal opportunity obscures the reality that people do not in fact have equal opportunities and cannot always compete equally on their own. There is often disagreement between those who think that everyone should be independent and the government should stay out of people's lives as much as possible, and those who think that the government should step in to correct inequalities. For example, in France in 1982 and Italy in 1993, laws were passed requiring that a certain percentage of candidates for political office be women. But in both countries, the courts struck down the laws, saying

From Democracy to Dictatorship

In 1919, after Germany's defeat in World War I and a successful revolution that overturned the German **monarchy**, a democratic government was established. Over the next decade, Germany became a flourishing center of artistic and intellectual activity.

But with the beginning of the Great **Depression** in 1929, resentment over harsh restrictions placed on Germany by the treaty that ended World War I resurfaced. Blame fell on the government. The National **Socialist** German Workers', or Nazi, Party fanned the flames of that resentment and used it to win votes. In 1933, the Nazi party gained control of the German **parliament**, and Adolf Hitler became the chancellor, or head, of the government. Parliament passed a law that gave Hitler power to ignore the constitution and to issue decrees that had the same force as laws. When the German president died in 1934, Hitler added the presidential powers to those of the chancellor and took control of the country. Germany had become a dictatorship.

Before their defeat in 1945, Hitler and the Nazis would be responsible for some of the most terrible and tragic acts the world has ever known, including the Holocaust—the systematic killing of 11 million people, including 6 million Jews.

French philosopher Voltaire

that they violated constitutional protections for equality (although in 2000, the French legislature changed the French constitution to include the percentage requirement). Several other countries, including Belgium and Argentina, have had such laws in place since the 1990s.

Even if the citizens are well equipped to govern themselves and sufficient equality exists, one concern is that people will not have the time or the desire to get involved in their government. French philosopher François-Marie Arouet (1694–1778), better known by his pen name, Voltaire, warned that "so long as the people do not care to exercise their freedom," it will be possible for someone to seize power and deny people their rights; it is easy "to put shackles upon sleeping men." Hitler's rise to power in Nazi Germany was a prime example of this. But Alexis de Tocqueville (1805–59), a French political scientist and historian, had an answer for Voltaire: at least in a democracy, he pointed out, people have a choice.

When you give people freedom, you take the risk that they will use that freedom to do things you think they should not do—such as not bothering to vote, or saying terrible things about other people. But when everyone has freedom, everyone has the power to do something about the things they do not like. You can encourage people to vote, and protest against things with which you disagree. Winston Churchill (1874–1965), the British prime minister during World War II, noted: "No one pretends that democracy is perfect or all-wise. Indeed, it has been said that democracy is the worst form of government except all those other forms that have been tried from time to time."

Is True Democracy Possible?

Jean-Jacques Rousseau was a Swiss-French philosopher and author. His 1762 book *The Social Contract* greatly influenced ideas about democracy. He struggled with the problem of creating a practical government based on lofty ideals:

"If we take the term in the strict sense, there never has been a real democracy, and there never will be. It is against the natural order for the many to govern and the few to be governed. It is unimaginable that the people should remain continually assembled to devote their time to public affairs, and it is clear that they cannot set up commissions for that purpose without the form of administration being changed.

"In fact, … when the functions of government are shared by several tribunals, the less numerous sooner or later acquire the greatest authority, if only because they are in a position to expedite affairs, and power thus naturally comes into their hands. …

"Were there a people of gods, their government would be democratic. So perfect a government is not for men."

Democracy in Action

The first known democracies were established in Athens and other ancient Greek cities. During the seventh century B.C., the Athenian nobles took power from the kings who traditionally ruled the city. The new government was run by several officials called *archons*, who were chosen from among the noble families. In 594 B.C., a poet and military commander named Solon (c. 638–558

OPPOSITE: Illustration of Athenian statesman Solon

B.C.) became an archon. He began changing many of the laws to make Athens more democratic.

Solon transferred many functions and powers of government from the Areopagus, a council of nobles who served life terms, to the Council of 400, an assembly of citizens serving one-year terms. Previously, political participation was restricted to people from noble families. Solon divided citizens into four classes and changed the laws so that all but those in the poorest class could serve in the Council of 400. Under Solon's reforms, the Council wrote the laws, and the Assembly, a governing body in which any citizen could participate, voted on them.

Another famous Athenian, Cleisthenes (c. 570–508 B.C.), took Solon's reforms farther in 508 B.C. He divided Athenians into 10 tribes based on where they lived. Each tribe had 50 representatives in a Council of 500, similar to Solon's Council of 400. Any free man could be in the council regardless of wealth, and the representatives were chosen each year in a lottery. Through the reforms of Solon and Cleisthenes, the government of Athens changed from one based on nobility to a system aimed at ensuring that the interests of many diverse groups of people would be equally represented.

Athenian democracy was different from modern concepts of democracy in that it was not founded upon the idea that every person has an innate right to be free. For the Athenians, freedom was created through citizens' active participation in government. They believed that laws were a gift from the gods, and humans had a responsibility to maintain them. In modern democracies, however, people can choose whether to participate in government or to sit back and not get involved. Individual rights are not something that the government gives to the people; the people already have their rights, and the government does not have the power to take them away. This idea of innate rights developed in Europe during the Middle Ages (c. A.D. 500–1453).

In 1215, English nobles who had grown tired of constant disagreements with the king demanded that he give them a guarantee that their interests would be protected. King John (c. 1166–1216) consented to the Magna Carta, one of the most important documents in the history of democracy. It granted certain rights to all free men and placed limits on how government officials could behave. One of its most important guarantees established the right of all free men to be judged by their fellow citizens under the law before being imprisoned or having their property taken away.

The Magna Carta, signed by King John

This was an important advance, but democracy in England evolved slowly over time. During the 13th century, the kings began assembling nobles to advise them on legislative and policy matters, decide disputes, and grant relief to petitioners. By the end of the 14th century, these councils had become a more formal and permanent body known as Parliament. Then, in the 15th century, Parliament became very powerful when its approval became required in order to make laws.

But power struggles and disagreements between Parliament and the king went on for centuries, even sparking a civil war in 1642. By the 19th century, much of the power had shifted from the king to Parliament; most importantly, the choice of prime minister became the right of Parliament. Today, the prime minister is the head of government, and the king or queen has only a ceremonial role. Members of one part of Parliament, the House of Lords, are chosen by the prime minister and serve for life, and members of the other part, the House of Commons, are elected by the people they represent.

The development of democracy took several leaps forward during the 18th century. The ideas of Rousseau, Voltaire, Scotsman David Hume (1711–76), and French philosopher Charles-Louis de Secondat, better known as Montesquieu (1689–1755), revolutionized how people thought about government. Their writings established the principles of democracy that are almost taken for granted today. In 1787, American **colonists**, newly free of British rule following the American Revolution, made use of their ideas to launch a grand experiment in democratic government.

From the beginning, the Americans were democratically inclined, although this was more by chance than by choice. As colonists separated from their government by a wide ocean, Americans had long been ruling themselves to a large extent. They were already used to voting, petitioning, engaging in public debates, and demonstrating. Moreover, they began as 13 separate colonies; this was the perfect recipe for representative government when they decided, in 1787, to form one nation. Finally, they had just fought a revolution in large part because they

George Washington at the signing of the Constitution in 1787

were denied representation in the British Parliament, so they were keenly aware that representation was an important aspect of just government.

The group of men who met to plan the new national government created a system that separated the powers of government and balanced them against each other. This was necessary in order to satisfy the representatives of all 13 colonies, none of whom wanted to give up power, and because they believed it was essential to preserving the independence that they had fought a revolution to achieve. One way that they created this delicate balance was by giving some powers to the colonies, now called states, and some powers to the national, or federal, government.

The system America's founding fathers established remains in place today. The federal government can check, or limit, the power of the states through its judicial branch, which can strike down state laws if they violate the federal Constitution. The states, in turn, can control the federal government through the federal legislative branch, or Congress, which is made up of representatives of the states. The balance of power among the different states is maintained through the organization of the legislative branch: one part of Congress, the Senate, has two representatives, or senators, from each state. The number of representatives in the other part, the House

Justifying Revolution

In 1776, British colonists in America announced their intention to separate from Great Britain and rule themselves in the Declaration of Independence. The colonists justified their revolutionary action on democratic principles:

"We hold these truths to be self-evident, that all men are created equal, that they are endowed by their Creator with certain unalienable Rights, that among these are Life, Liberty, and the pursuit of Happiness.—That to secure these rights, Governments are instituted ... deriving their just powers from the consent of the governed,—That ... it is the Right of the People to alter or to abolish it, and to institute new Government, laying its foundation on such principles and organizing its powers in such form, as to them shall seem most likely to effect their Safety and Happiness.... When a long train of abuses ... pursuing invariably the same Object evinces a design to reduce them under absolute **Despotism**, it is their right, it is their duty, to throw off such Government, and to provide new Guards.... Such has been the patient sufferance of these Colonies; and such is now the necessity which constrains them to alter their former Systems of Government."

of Representatives, is proportional to a state's population. Heavily populated states such as California may have more representatives in the House (53) than smaller states such as Rhode Island (2), but the even numbers of the Senate prevent the House from taking too much control.

During the 20th century, many other nations adopted democratic forms of government, including France, Israel, and Japan. The rise in democratic systems of government created pressure on former colonial powers such as England and Spain to grant independence to their colonies in Africa and South America. Many of those newer nations, such as Ghana and Bolivia, set up democratic governments of their own.

Today, more than a third of the countries in the world are governed democratically. As democracy spreads, many people believe that governments that are already democratic should actively try to build democracies in other countries. But democracy by nature requires the involvement of the people; it is not something that can be imposed from the outside. For example, the U.S. encountered many difficulties and setbacks in its attempt to establish democracy in Afghanistan after the 2001 defeat of the Taliban, a religious dictatorship that was sponsoring terrorism.

Some people argue that the difficulties encountered in Afghanistan and elsewhere are because democracy is a **Western** idea that may not work in other cultures. Others believe that democracy is a truly universal ideal and that everyone should have the opportunity to enjoy its freedoms. Regardless of how it is carried out, most people agree that everyone has the right to participate in his or her government.

Another difficult question facing governments in the 21st century is how to create democracy on an international level. Currently, there are large imbalances of power between wealthier nations and less developed nations in international organizations such as the UN and the World Trade Organization. More than 2,600 years after the first democracy began, new challenges continue to arise. A new generation of democratic thinkers has stood up to meet them, and the concept of democracy continues to evolve.

Timeline

594 B.C. The first democracy is established in Athens through the legal reforms of Solon and Cleisthenes.

335 B.C. Aristotle establishes his school in Athens.

A.D. 930 The first national legislative assembly, the Althing, is created in Iceland.

1215 King John issues the Magna Carta in response to demands from English nobles.

1642 Civil war breaks out in England after King Charles I refuses to give Parliament greater power.

1762 Swiss-French philosopher Jean-Jacques Rousseau publishes *The Social Contract*.

1775 British colonists in North America revolt and set up an independent, democratic government.

1831 French historian Alexis de Tocqueville visits the U.S. to observe its democratic government in action.

1861 Civil war erupts in the U.S. after 11 southern states declare their independence.

1867 Four British colonies approve a democratic constitution forming the Confederation of Canada but keep ties to Britain.

1923 The democratic republic of Turkey is established, ending more than 600 years of rule by the Ottoman Empire.

1933 Adolf Hitler becomes chancellor of newly democratic Germany and establishes a dictatorship.

1947 The Japanese constitution is ratified, establishing a democratic government.

1948 The UN unanimously adopts the Universal Declaration of Human Rights.

1948 Israel establishes itself as an independent nation and sets up a democratic government.

1958 France adopts a constitution establishing a democratic government.

1960 The UN adopts a resolution encouraging colonial powers to grant independence to their territories.

1963 The Organization of African Unity is established, in part to promote independence from colonial powers. (Disbanded in 2002, it was replaced by the African Union.)

1991 The Union of Soviet Socialist Republics breaks up; several new nations, including Latvia and Lithuania, form democracies.

2004 Citizens of Afghanistan vote in the country's first democratic election for president.

Selected Bibliography

Crick, Bernard. *Democracy: A Very Short Introduction*. New York: Oxford University Press, 2002.

Dahl, Robert A. *On Democracy*. New Haven, Conn.: Yale University Press, 1998.

Encyclopedia Britannica. *The New Encyclopedia Britannica*. Chicago: Encyclopedia Britannica, 2005.

Wiebe, Robert H. *Self-Rule: A Cultural History of American Democracy*. Chicago: University of Chicago Press, 1995.

World Book Encyclopedia. *The World Book Encyclopedia*. Chicago: World Book, 2006.

Glossary

bureaucracy a huge, complex system of government with many rules and many people with specialized functions

colonists people who travel to a distant place and establish a new community but are still governed by their home country

communism a system of government that discourages private ownership of property and enterprise; instead, the government manages property and enterprise on behalf of its citizens

constitution	the basic ideas by which a country is governed, particularly as they relate to the powers of government and the rights of citizens
depression	a period of economic difficulty marked by excessive unemployment, high prices, and low wages
despotism	another term for dictatorship
dictatorship	a government ruled by one person with absolute power (a dictator), usually a tyrant who abuses his or her power and oppresses people
economic	relating to the production and distribution of wealth; countries with strong economies often have wealthier citizens than those with weak economies
human rights	rights believed to belong universally to every person, such as the right to live and to speak freely without fear of detention or torture from a government
jury	a group of ordinary citizens who have sworn to be fair and uphold the law; they are assembled to listen to a case in court and make a judgment on it
monarchy	a government in which the power is held by one person who rules for life and who has inherited the position, usually from his or her parent

nobles in some societies, the name given to a class of people who are regarded as socially superior, often because of connections to wealth or royalty but also from their family associations

parliament a group of officials elected to make laws in a country; many countries in Europe have a parliament

petitions formal requests for an authority to take certain actions; petitions to a court may be a complaint or lawsuit against another party, or an appeal of a decision by another government authority

republic a form of government in which government officials represent citizens; republics are often, but not always, democratic

socialist relating to a system of government based on government-run enterprise; communism goes one step beyond socialism, as its goal is to progress to public ownership of enterprise and all aspects of government

sovereign possessing absolute, supreme power or authority; self-governing; in a monarchy, the monarch is sovereign and the people are his or her subjects, whereas in a democracy, the people are sovereign

transparency openness; a transparent government is conducted publicly rather than in secret, in a manner that permits everyone to see and understand what is being done

trying examining or investigating through judicial procedures, such as reviewing evidence and hearing arguments presented by at least two opposing sides, in order to make a decision

unanimous having the consent of everyone; with all members in complete agreement

unbiased not influenced by opinions, prejudices, or a particular viewpoint; impartial and fair to all perspectives

uncensored not subject to review, editing, or approval by the government; free from the suppression of ideas and content

Western of the West, or the developed nations in western Europe and North America; often implies countries with democratic governments

Index